Dedication

To my friends who struggle

Table of Contents

Introduction: We all Dream 4

Budgeting: The Mindset 6

Truth About Debt 7

Re-evaluation: 10

On What Are You Spending Your Money? 10

Analyze Your Current Situation 11

Nonrecurring Expenses 13

Recurring Expenses 14

Your Lifestyle and Budgeting 15

Money Saving Methods and Tips 16

Saving Money of Groceries 19

How to Save Up on Clothing 20

Saving Money: Family Activities 21

Decorating and Home Furnishings 22

Cheap Travelling and Holiday Spending 23

Saving Money on The Internet and Mobile Devices 24

Bills: Paying less for Energy 26

Lights and Electronics 26

Digital Thermostat 28

Budgeting: Story of My Friend 29

Take Action: How To Change Your Mindset and Start Budgeting 31

Final Word 33

Huge Thank You and Words of Gratitude! 34

Copyright 35

Disclaimer 35

Introduction:

We all Dream

„A budget tells us what we can't afford, but it doesn't keep us from buying it."

William Feather

Most people have dreams, small or large; they have dreams. You might wish to travel around the world, seeing ancient and historic sites. Another person may dream of owning a five-bedroom house, with matching furniture, and raising two kids. Your goals are important to you, but life requires money.

Unless you have a steady income, savings, and a budget for how to spend that money, you will have difficulty attaining some of your dreams. You certainly will not be happy if you cannot achieve all your goals.

It does not matter how old you are, you need to have a budget. You need to know what your expenses are, what your income is, and what you can save to ensure you can pay for the bigger ticket items you want.

You could also change your desires and would like to live a minimalist lifestyle. True happiness does not come from being a millionaire. Happiness comes from accepting what you have and the people around you.

If you can accept what is around you and stop being disappointed in what you don't have—you will find happiness.

Budgeting is a way to look at your lifestyle as it is and discover how to make improvements. Understanding how to budget will ensure that you can work towards some of the things you actually want.

This beginner's guide will help teach you how to stay out of debt, how to save your money, and provide you with a "start now" plan to get your financial life on track.

Budgeting begins with a psychological change within yourself. The first step to getting a budget and saving money—is recognizing what you do that inhibits your ability to reach what you desire. Are you the type of person to make a purchase in the now?

Perhaps, you can wait and save, before buying a big ticket item? Most individuals who are looking at a book about budgeting tend to buy what they want now, instead of waiting. Others are looking for a way to extend what little money they have, by learning tricks they have not thought of.

The answers are right here at your fingertips. You will discover how to save money on expenses, as well as the psychology of waiting for what you want.

Budgeting: The Mindset

„The budget is not just a collection of numbers, but an expression of our values and aspirations."

Jacob Lew

Budgeting requires a proper mindset. It's based on an understanding of good and bad debt. Everything rests on the goals you have in mind and what will make you content in life.

Reaching true contentment is difficult. It doesn't happen overnight, but there are ways to curb your desires. There are ways to alleviate the jealousies you may feel over what other people have.

The best lesson that can be offered is to realize the more expectations and desires you have, the more disappointed you will feel when something does not go well.

The truth about suffering in life is having desires rooted in material goods and pleasures. To end your suffering, you have to stop living a mundane life. Happiness comes from those who are in your life and the pleasures you take in simple things.

Truth About Debt

„You can't be in debt and win. It doesn't work."

Dave Ramsey

Debt is rarely something you can avoid. There are purchases in life that could take you decades to make if secured loans did not exist. However, there are also debts that reflect poorly on your credit report, if you miss payments. These bad debts are unsecured, and the easiest to obtain. You might be familiar with them—credit cards.

Credit card companies make it incredibly appealing to take out a card, increase the credit limit, and spend money. Unfortunately, the high APRs (annual percentage rates) make credit cards highly dangerous to your monetary situation.

Taking on Debt

In life, you will probably have one or more of the following:

- Student loans

- Car Loan

- Mortgage

- Medical bills

- Tax Payments

- Credit Cards

Tax payments may occur if you have not withheld enough taxes from your paycheck or if you run your own business. A tax bill is a bad debt to have because the government penalizes you for late payments. You may be in a cycle of paying your tax debt for more than three years, depending on how much you can allocate towards the payment each month. It is not a comfortable situation.

Credit cards are a crutch. Not only can you spend more than you have a need to pay, but credit cards make it easy to do so. Once you get into the cycle of paying with a credit card, the only way to stop is to cut them up and never get another card.

Student loans, car loans, mortgages, and medical bills are a part of life. To have a decent career that will pay you a livable wage, you have to go to a university or college. Most employers are not going to look at you if you have not attended a trade school, college, or university.

Transportation is imperative, but do you need a vehicle? It depends on where you live. If you reside in a place without a bus system or other public transportation, then you need a car, bike, or to walk. Walking cuts into the time you spend with your family and earn money, on the other hand, it is healthy for you. There are pros and cons, and you have to determine if the pros of having a vehicle outweigh the $20,000 to $40,000 debt you would undertake.

Everyone needs a place to live. Do you have to gain a mortgage? No, but there are more advantages to owning a home than renting a place. These benefits will be mentioned under "planning for significant expenses."

Medical expenses are also something you cannot avoid. Even with the insurance marketplace that was started a few years ago, you still have the possibility of incurring high medical debts. It is an unavoidable expense you can plan for.

Re-evaluation:

On What Are You Spending Your Money?

You have to be very analytical and truthful when you assess how you spend. You will write down what you make and what you spend. It will help you see the black and white of it all, but you also need to go deeper now.

If you overspent last month, why did you do so? Were you overly stressed? Did you feel tired that you could not buy what you wanted? Were you frustrated? Did you think you had the money to spend but did not sit down to analyze your budget and all that needed to be paid? Did you forget about a bill?

Analyzing your current spending habits, along with the emotions you are feeling • will help you determine what you need to do to correct your mindset.

How do you want to spend your money?

What is your ideal situation, with the money you are making now? What are your goals? What do you hope for later in life, as well as when you reach retirement? Are these goals materialistic or are they something that will make you happy to the point that you can keep to your budget?

What will force you stick to your budget?

Analyze Your Current Situation

What gets measured, gets managed.

Before you can change your life or create a budget for your current circumstance, you will need to assess your whole situation.

Have you written down all of your income, expenses, miscellaneous expenses, and infrequent expenses? Most individuals go through their mind, a list of what needs to be paid and when. They do not sit down and look at their financial situation in black and white. If you have not done this, then you need to do so. There should be three categories for your list:

• Income and Additional Income

• Recurring Expenses

• Nonrecurring Expenses Income and Additional Income

For income, you should only write down what is absolute. Yes, there is a potential that your situation could change within the year. A person could lose their job. But, for budgeting purposes, you are going to assume that your job is secure. You will want to list your gross and net income.

Secondly, if there are many household incomes, list all of them.

If you have a part time job, make sure this revenue is listed, regardless of whether you pay taxes on that money or not. If you do not work each week at this secondary job, then do not count it. For example, if you babysit four days out of the month and !mow this will not change you can write it down. However, if you never know when you will have income from a secondary job, then you should not include it.

For self-employed individuals, it is much harder to set up a budget in the same manner as a full-time career with a salary or hourly wage. Each month can be a different income.

For self-employed people, you needed to use last years reported gross income to determine a budget. You might not make as much this year, as last, so after the first quarter, you will need to re-evaluate your budget. You will need to determine your first four months' average income, and plan accordingly.

Nonrecurring Expenses

These are expenses that occur throughout the year but may not happen next year. For example, if your dishwasher broke and you replaced it last year, you won't budget for it this year.

You can plan for these things, to a degree. For example, if you bought your water heater 30 years ago, chances are in a year or two, you will need money to replace it. If the roof on your home was replaced 25 years ago, with 20- year shingles you need to budget for a new roof.

If you bought tires five years ago, then have the amount of tread left on the tires, checked and determine how much longer you can drive on those tires.

You can always get information for most non-recurring expenses.

Colds, flu, other illnesses, and emergent situations are things you cannot plan for. You can't say, well this year a snow storm is going to cause a tree to break a window.

While you cannot predict emergent situations and illnesses, you can still set a budget. Knowledge is very powerful.

Recurring Expenses

These are expenses that happen every month, every quarter, or every year. For example, electricity, water, sewer, gas, internet, phone, and TV, are usually the top recurring expenses. Student loan, mortgage, and car loan payments are also recurring.

You can split this category into two: unchanging and average costs. Unchanging expenses are mortgages and student loans. You know each month you must pay a specific amount. It will not change.

Average fees are utility bills. Each month depends on your usage, so from month to month the bill can change a few dollars to over $100. Like changing income, you have to average the monthly bills to determine what you will payout for the year. In a month, you will budget for $100 on electricity, but the bill is $40 so that $70 extra remains in the power budget and when the bill becomes $150 in winter due to heating expenses, you have the extra $50 from the over-budgeting you did in a summer month.

Even groceries can be averaged per month to help you spend less on food and household items. It just takes more time mastering how you spend what you allocate for groceries.

Your Lifestyle and Budgeting

There are certain things many of us do not contemplate as we are setting up our adult lives. Yes, you plan for a particular career by gaining education to work in that industry. However, you cannot always plan for the job you obtain. You might work in one field for five years, switch to a new area, or get a promotion that moves you half way across the country.

As you assess your current situation, you need to have a hard look at the cost of living in your area. You can do this by looking at websites and Forbes magazine. There are quite a few places that have started making a cost of living comparisons.

You can assess where you live versus other cities and towns in the same state, as well as nationwide. It is a good idea to evaluate these concepts if you can make your living situation better. Self-employed individuals, typically freelancers who can move around and not be in the same location to help their clients, have the option of turning to a place that offers a better cost of living for their income.

Assess the cost of living, where you live, and determine if your career could be offering you a better salary.

Money Saving Methods and Tips

Assessing your current situation helps you see just how much you spend on certain expenses. It is the best way to start determining where you can save money and significantly impact your happiness in life, by reaching the goals you have set. The following are a few of the areas, where you could actually save money or even make money.

Groceries and Related Expenses

By far, food cost are one of the largest ticket items that recurs each month, so you can survive. It is also an area that everyone overlooks for cutting back. There are three areas, where you can save money on groceries and related expenses.

Eating Out

Dining out is expensive and relatively unhealthy. Most restaurants overuse salt, making it dangerous to your health. You also tend to eat more calories when you eat out. Here are some suggestions for reducing your dining out expenses:

- Share a meal with another family member. This reduces your portion size; plus, reduces the amount you pay.

- Choose restaurants with healthier options, such as a diabetic menu or gluten free menu.

- Choose 4 places, you want to eat out per month. Choose one day a week to eat at one of these locations. Basically, choose your top 4 favorite restaurants or if you have many places you love to eat, rotate eating at these locations.

- Limit yourself to one coffee from a store per week.

- Stop having coffee at noon, every day. This will remove the caffeine from your system, and help you sleep better.

- Sleep better at night by establishing a new routine. Turn off all electronics 30 minutes prior to sleep, avoid caffeine and chocolate, and read a book or meditate.

- Increase your exercise because sleeping better, getting more exercise, and not overindulging in coffee will help increase your energy, so you will cook at home. Buying Household Items

Toilet paper, tissues, cleaning supplies, dish detergent, dishwasher soap, and laundry detergent should be an every 3 to 4-month purchase. These are items you can buy in bulk from warehouse stores. Buying small bottles means you spend more throughout the year.

Cleaning supplies are the biggest waste people spend money on. What is a Clorox wipe? It is nothing more than a hardy, moist towel placed in scented bleach. Water and vinegar is also a great combination for cleaning hardwood, tile, linoleum, and walls. It is a recipe of ingredients your ancestors used and it costs less than $3 to $5 a bottle for cleaning supplies that can harm the environment.

To be honest, medical supplies can also be something you save on. There are numerous medicinal herbs you can raise to help heal cuts, sanitize wounds, and even eat a healthier meal. If you do buy medical supplies, then go to the Dollar Store Usually the ingredients are the same, the only difference is the price. Reading labels will help you to save your hard-earned money.

It is going to take time to learn what you can and cannot purchase for less, but once you do, you can save money on household items.

Saving Money of Groceries

Eating healthy means eating cheaply. Yes, fruits and some vegetables can become expensive depending on where you live and where they are imported from. However, you will have fewer medical bills by eating healthy and ignoring the frozen and canned food section. People who have switched to a non-gluten diet also feel more energized

There will be certain things that are more expensive, but in the end, if the healthy food is more expensive you will have fewer medical bills later on.

Coupons also exist. Buy a newspaper, sign up for coupon sites like All You, and take advantage of these valuable coupons. You will spend more on cake mix, cookies, and other unhealthy foods if you use coupons. However, when and if there are coupons for healthy foods like yogurt, you can save money. Find the best deals.

My advice is to buy groceries directly from the warehouse, not from a supermarket. It does require good communication skills when approaching the staff there. If you are lucky, you can pay 50% less. If anyone of your friends, relatives work in the factory, you can always ask for discount products. The more you buy from places like this, cheaper it will be.

How to Save Up on Clothing

„The best way to look stylish on a budget is to try second-hand, bargain hunting, and vintage."

Orlando Bloom

Many people spend too much on clothing. There is a cycle to retail. Unless, a pair of pants, shirt, underwear, socks, or other clothing has a hole, start getting into the retail cycle for buying items.

Yes, designer stuff is wonderful, but you can find some pretty great outfits at outlet stores for half the cost. You can even get name brands at certain shops. In retail, clothing is always brought in ahead of the coming season. Half-way through a new season, the sales start and by the end of the season you can get clothing that is 50% or more off. By getting into the cycle of buying clothing during these sales, you can lower your clothing expenses and improve your budget.

Furthermore, if you do feel a need to buy new clothing, then start an online store. Sell your old clothing that is in good shape, so you recoup some of your expenditure on your clothing. Even if you have a garage sale and get rid of most of your clothing, you can recover a few dollars.

Saving Money: Family Activities

No one wants to stay home all the time. Yes, it can be fun to play a game, have family movie night, and run around the lawn or backyard. There are so many things you can experience in life. You don't always want to stay home.

There are ways to enjoy family activities without killing the budget. For example, if you go to a movie, just purchase the movie tickets. Most theaters have a cup they can provide for free for water. It may not seem fun to avoid concessions, but honestly, the costs are just too high. The markup on concessions is extremely high so that the theater can make a profit. The cost of tickets is set to cover the cost of bringing the movie to the stage. In fact, movie theaters break even on their expenses for the film, labor, and overhead through the movie tickets. If a movie doesn't perform then, the concessions usually ensure the theater can remain open.

The point is, for family activities, you can save money by being smart. If you have a zoo in your hometown or close, you can pay for membership, go to the zoo often, and take a picnic lunch versus buying a meal there.

You can also search your local listings for free events, such as music festivals, movies, rodeos, arts and crafts, wool markets, and other activities. If you have children, then educating your children about these events is important, even if you find them annoying. If there are any parks, campgrounds, or coupons to places, then go for the inexpensive fun.

Decorating and Home Furnishings

The number one rule on home furnishings and decorating is to sell your current items for as much as you can get. Make sure you are getting money for your old items, unless they are extremely dirty or damaged. If no one is willing to pay, then get the right off for donating the items.

Like with de-cluttering your home, you want to stick with the rule—if you bring something new in, then something else must go, preferably for a little cash.

If you have decorations that you are tired of for the holidays, try to sell what you have before you buy new things.

Shop smart. Certain furniture stores don't provide quality. In a year or even less that expensive item can break down or become damaged. Shop in a place that offers a good product for the value. If you do have an issue, call, use the warranty, and get it replaced. Don't let things like warranties go because they are there for any problems that arise, at least with reputable stores.

If you want to change your decorating scheme, look around, shop, and then make purchases. One store can have the same item, but for more or in some cases less than another.

Cheap Travelling and Holiday Spending

„The cold harsh reality is that we have to balance the budget."

Michael Bloomberg

Holiday spending is an area where you can save. You are not being told to go to the seedy hotel on the outskirts of the projects, but to find a package that is all-inclusive and reasonable. You don't have to stay in a multimillion dollar resort, where celebrities hang out. You can choose a modest hotel and be comfortable. You can also elect to do the top most important things, versus trying to do everything and spending more than you need to.

Some packages include a day at this park, a day at another park, and so on. One of the best ways to spend less on holidays you set up is to ask local forums about things to do.

Don't go to any popular hotel searching sites. Instead, find a forum that is created by locals, where they talk about cool things they have done in their home town. You can find things that are inexpensive. Or join Facebook group related to travelling, trust me there will be many people who will want to help you.

Research is the key to spending wisely on a holiday.

Saving Money on The Internet and Mobile Devices

Another area you can save money on your internet and mobile devices. It is also an area that has become one of the greatest expenses in our lives. We cannot seem to forgo the electronic world and technology now that we have it. We are also creating a dependency on it. There is a whole movement called, unplugging, where people get off the grid, away from technology, and enjoy a few weeks or the rest of their life without the "must haves" of today's era.

It's understandable that you may not be able to unplug all the time. If you have a job where you are on call over the weekends and evenings, then you can't distance yourself, but that does not mean you shouldn't save money on your expenses.

Internet

Internet companies attempt to sell you the highest megabytes per second downloading speed they can. They are in the business of making money off their service. But, you do not have to buy into the jargon. Yes, streaming TV, running multiple online shows, and computers on the internet is better with a faster speed. However, you can also unplug the kids from multiple devices and have family time.

The average household can survive on 12 Mbps downloading speeds for multiple devices. It may require a little buffering depending on the amount of electronics using the internet and whether you are on a busy IP address, with other users. However, the internet is built so that multiple people use the same IP network, which is why 12 Mbps can be enough for your regular usage.

You also have the option of bundling your services with most companies. You could bundle your mobile phone, internet and TV for a lower price than having each one individually.

Bills: Paying less for Energy

Another expense that many people spend a great deal on is energy to keep their house air conditioned or heated. It's an expense that we tend to feel we cannot do anything about.

However, it is simply not true. There are a lot of things you can do to lower your energy bills. It takes changing your mindset and using self-discipline.

Lights and Electronics

One of the biggest areas that people waste money on regarding energy is on their lights and electronics. If you do not know how much your items draw, there are places to find out, as well as tools you can use to see how much energy you are drawing.

Certain items cannot be unplugged: fridges, stoves, washing machines, and dryers. The plugs are too inconvenient. For some houses, a microwave can be difficult to unplug.

In my opinion, anything else that is readily available should be unplugged when it is not in use, For example, remove the plug from the outlet, not just from the device. If you have a tablet and you, need to charge it, charge it and then remove the plug from the wall.

Lights are another example. If you are not in a room or reading, then don't have every light on in the house. Have one energy efficient lamp in each room for reading or watching TV.

Unplug your TV. Even off, your TV is drawing quite a bit of power.

If you own your home, think about installing solar panels. It is an expense at first, but the 20 to $30 bills you get all year round makes up for the installation costs.

There are two things these things can do for you. The first is to reduce heat escaping in the winter. If you live in the mountains, northern states, or other cold places, then you want to have window coverings. Windows are designed to breathe a little, so air can leak in making your heater system work overtime.

Leave the window coverings down, except when the sun is coming around to provide warmth. On days where the temperatures are below 30 degrees Fahrenheit, leave the window coverings down.

If you live with a lot of windows and plenty of sun, in the summer, you may find you are using a lot of air conditioning simply because you are leaving the window coverings open. More suggestions can be made, but basically, find out what you can do in your home to reduce energy-using window coverings.

Digital Thermostat

"If you don't have the money management skills yet, using a debit card will ensure you don't overspend and rack up debt on a credit card."

H. Eker

A digital thermostat that you can set to a particular temperature is going to reduce your expenses. You can set your home to a warmer or cooler temperature while you are at work. Why have a constant 68 to 72 degrees Fahrenheit in your home, if you are not going to be there? Instead, turn it down to 65.

An hour before you come home, have the thermostat set to increase to your ideal temperature. When you go to bed, studies have proven that a cooler room is better for sleeping. With a digital thermostat, you can control your expenses and thus have a better budget for the things you do want. I still remember using thermostat when I was younger.

Budgeting: Story of My Friend

A little about the mindset you have has been discussed, but now it is time to determine truly the things you can do to improve the psychology of your spending. These will help as you analyze the "start now" budgeting plan.

How we are raised can in part determine how we spend money now. Psychological concerns and stress can lead some individuals to spend money incorrectly.

A young woman was raised without her family having a lot of money. She was also the last of 4 children. She was depressed, no eating out, and no toys that were truly her own. When she grew up, she was very stressed whenever she did not have enough money to pay for items. In fact, she would go out on spending sprees buying clothing and other items because she "deserved" to have a little fun and live a life, even though she could not afford it. She was "tired of not being able to enjoy life," even after working so hard for the little income she could make. She knew she should not spend the money, but she could not stop herself.

This young woman's husband would put a cushion in her account. He would put $500 in the account, but not let her see the bank statements or record it in her checking account register. She was always safe to spend money, and was told to spend some money on herself, and she would. Occasionally, she would overspend, but there was the cushion on her account.

You can have parents that provide you with many things, but teach you responsible spending, and you can still overspend your income. You can also have parents who spend and spend, buying you whatever you want, and you figure you can do the same because you weren't taught responsibility.

If you can understand the psychology behind your spending habits from your upbringing, then you can start to change your mindset.

Take Action: How To Change Your Mindset and Start Budgeting

Once you have assessed your upbringing, current spending habits, and how you wish to spend your money in the future, you are ready to follow the tasks outlined here:

- Write your short-term goals on a poster board.

- List the short-term goals by cost and importance.

- Write down your long-term goals.

- List these aims by value, importance, and the reasonable date of reaching that goal.

- Assess the list, are there things you don't need or actually want, but think you would like to have? Sometimes we want something because we see it, and it sounds great, but after thinking about it, we know it will sit and gather dust for 75% of the time. Motorcycles, gaming consoles and other products tend to sit more often than they are used because of our busy lives.

- Remove anything that you do not think you will have time to enjoy.

- Now assess your list goals again, determine if you want to re-order anything in the order of importance. Do so if it needs to be changed. Otherwise, you are now ready to post this board somewhere you will see it. You want to look at this board each day. Take a picture so it is on your phone too.

- When you go shopping, pull out your phone, look at the short and long term goals you have. Is there something in your cart that you can forgo buying to save up for the actual goals you have? For example, if you are buying brownie mix that is $4.50 is it more important to you than one of your short or long term goals? Yes, $4.50 is not much, but what if you pick that product up each time you go shopping? Let's say it is a latte for $4.50 and you get one each week. Imagine if you are buying a latte for $4.50 on a daily basis! **That's a lot**. Now let's face reality. You could do a lot with this money, you could travel or maybe start your own business.

Final Word

You can see from just determining what you are spending and assessing your real goals, how you can begin to change your mindset.

A dose of reality is often the best way for you to limit how much you spend on items in the now versus saving up for the things you truly want. Yes, it is nice to spend money on something you want as a new blouse because it makes you look great, but need versus want is what truly determines if you reach your ultimate life goals.

1. Re-evaluate your emotions and your desires to spend money now versus on your goals later on
2. Look at your goals every time you want to buy something you want versus need • Take a breath or ten breaths
3. Analyze your emotions, your stress level, and why you feel you must have it
4. Set your goals
5. Take a picture of those goals or have them in your wallet
6. Use meditation at home to release your stress and feelings of 'deserving" something special

Huge Thank You and Words of Gratitude!

First and foremost, Thank You for downloading this book. At the end of the day I'm **extremely** grateful for **every** download and **every** purchase. It really makes me smile and motivates me. I wish that every person would put their best forward for the human race. I wish you unlimited mental strength and discipline to achieve your goals and dreams. **Together** we can make the difference.

If you found the information useful I would be extremely grateful if you could write a short Amazon review. It really does make the difference and I personally read every review and take notes. I want to improve my books, so that I can provide more value to other people. I know that my future books will give you the best experience possible.

Copyright

Copyright 2016, all rights reserved. No part of this publication may be reproduced in any form or by any means, including scanning, photocopying, or otherwise without written permission of the author of this work.

Writer: Petyr J. Chekk

Publisher: Transcendence Publishing

Disclaimer

Disclaimer and Terms of Use: The Author takes no responsibility for errors, omissions, or contrary interpretation of the subject. Any perceived slights of specific persons, peoples are unintentional. In any advice book, like anything else in life, there are no guarantees made. The author is not liable for any damages and/or negative consequences as results of contents of this book.

www.ingramcontent.com/pod-product-compliance
Lightning Source LLC
Chambersburg PA
CBHW070424190526
45169CB00003B/1403